in Dark
Places

OMF International works in most East Asian countries, and among East Asian peoples around the world. It was founded by James Hudson Taylor in 1865 as the China Inland Mission. Our overall purpose is to glorify God through the urgent evangelisation of East Asia's billions, and this is reflected in our publishing.

Through our books, booklets, website and quarterly magazine, *East Asia's Billions*, OMF Publishing aims to motivate Christians for world mission, and to equip them for playing a part in it. Publications include:

- contemporary mission issues
- the biblical basis of mission
- the life of faith
- stories and biographies related to God's work in East Asia
- accounts of the growth and development of the church in Asia
- studies of Asian cultures and religion relating to the spiritual needs of her peoples

Visit our website at *www.omf.org*

Addresses for OMF English-speaking centres can be found at the back of this book.

[ courage >

in Dark Places

j an g reenough

MONARCH
BOOKS
Mill Hill, London & Grand Rapids, Michigan

Copyright © Jan Greenough 2002.
The right of Jan Greenough to be identified
as author of this work has been asserted by her in
accordance with the Copyright, Designs
and Patents Act 1988.

First published by Monarch Books in 2002,
Concorde House, Grenville Place,
Mill Hill, London NW7 3SA.

Published in conjunction with OMF.

Distributed by:
UK: STL, PO Box 300, Kingstown Broadway, Carlisle,
Cumbria CA3 0QS;
USA: Kregel Publications, PO Box 2607,
Grand Rapids, Michigan 49501.

ISBN 1 85424 584 8

All rights reserved.
No part of this publication may be reproduced or
transmitted in any form or by any means, electronic
or mechanical, including photocopy, recording or any
information storage and retrieval system, without
permission in writing from the publisher.

Unless otherwise stated, Scripture quotations are
taken from the Holy Bible, New International Version,
copyright © 1973, 1978, 1984 by the International Bible Society.
Used by permission of Hodder and Stoughton Ltd.
All rights reserved.

**British Library Cataloguing Data**
A catalogue record for this book is available
from the British Library

Book design and production for the publishers by
Gazelle Creative Productions Ltd,
Concorde House, Grenville Place, Mill Hill, London NW7 3SA.

# Contents

# Acknowledgements

David Michell, *A Boy's War*, OMF 1988.
Catherine L. Davis, *The Spirits of Mindoro*, OMF/
  Monarch Books 1998.

# Unsung Heroes

December 1942, Temple Hill Civilian Assembly Centre, north-eastern China. Rows of shivering children stand at attention, flanked by their weary teachers. They are cold, underfed and ragged, and they look anxiously at the Japanese commandant as he swaggers up with his attendant officers. "Numbers!" snaps an officer, and the roll-call begins.

*"Ichi, nee, san, she, go, roku!"* is what the soldiers hear. "Itchy knee; scratch a flea!" is what the first four children chant rapidly. The others giggle and continue with the rest of the Japanese numbers in a more orthodox fashion. It is a small rebellion, and the teachers smile quietly. In spite of all their hardships, a spark of mischief continues to shine in the children's eyes. The adults know that there are worse times ahead for all those interned in the Japanese occupation of China; they wonder if they will be able to pre-

serve any happiness or innocence for them in what is left of their childhood.

Every year the world remembers its war heroes: those who studied strategy and planned famous campaigns; those who led troops to victory; those who fought and died in battles. Yet there are many people who remember their own, more private heroes: people who remain largely unknown, but who survived the years of the Second World War with their faith and love intact, and who sheltered and cared for others with endless self-sacrifice. For the children of Chefoo School, their unsung heroes are the teachers who guarded and guided them with Christian love throughout their years as prisoners of war.

## The first journey

In the autumn of 1939 Japan was already threatening to invade China. On the other side of the world, Hitler's aggression had been met with a declaration of war by Great Britain. Soon, it seemed, the whole world would be at war. None of this was important to six-year-old David

Michell, who was facing a challenge of his own. He was about to leave his parents for the first time, to go to boarding-school.

His was no ordinary journey. His parents were Australian missionaries, working in Guiyang, capital of Guizhou province in central China. The school was Chefoo School, set up on the north-eastern coast of China to provide education in English for the children of missionaries (or MKs – missionary kids – as they were known). David was entrusted to the care of Chefoo staff for a 2,000-mile journey that would take six weeks, travelling by truck and train and boat, sometimes held up by bad weather, bad roads, or railway tracks destroyed by Japanese bombing.

It was January 1940 when David finally arrived at Chefoo to join his sister Joyce, on a day so cold that the ferry became frozen into the bay, and the children were transferred into rickshaws to cross the ice to the shore. David looked out of the rumbling cart, blinking in the icy wind. Ahead, he could see the square brick building of the preparatory school facing the beach, with a flight of steep steps leading up to the front doors.

Under his arm he clutched his parents' farewell present to him, a box of hand-carved wooden dominoes. They felt like his last link with home. He knew that he would see his parents again at the end of the school year. However, at six, he had scarcely any idea of how long that meant.

## School-days

School was an unfamiliar world, but the little boy settled quickly into the routine of lessons and play. The teaching staff were supported by house parents, who cared for the pupils outside lesson times; they were familiar with the early weeks of homesickness and knew how to comfort and distract the children, though discipline was firm and a certain British self-restraint, typical of the period, was encouraged. Lessons were based on the British education system, with older pupils taking Oxford matriculation exams, but in the prep school the international flavour of the pupils added extra interest. Many had been born in the country in which their parents were working, so they had a variety of Chinese dialects as their second languages. They also had to be prepared to return one day to their parents' home country, which meant being able to deal with the home currency; "money sums" could mean working in pounds, shillings and pence, US or Australian dollars, South African rands, Dutch guilders or Norwegian kroner – all in the same classroom. Even simple spellings had to be defined: "Please, how do you spell 'centre'? – I'm American."

On Saturdays, they played sports or went for outings to local beauty spots; in the summer, there were games on the beach and swimming in the sea. On Sunday mornings, the pupils lined up in pairs and paraded through the Chefoo streets to church; in the afternoon, their main recreation was another walk, often to the foreign cemetery, where they played hide-and-seek among the graves. At night, there was an official time for "lights out", but a dormitory full of seven-year-old boys was unlikely to be entirely peaceful: "dorm cricket" was played with a book and a rolled-up sock until a teacher came to investigate the noise; midnight feasts and story-telling in the dark made school life entertaining and eventful. David was happy enough.

The usual routine was for MKs to go home at the end of the year, but in 1940 travel was either too dangerous or (in some areas) not permitted by the authorities. The invading Japanese army was in charge in Chefoo town, where the Chinese schools had been forced to stop teaching English and replace it with Japanese, but no sanctions had as yet been imposed on the European community. Pat Bruce, the school's headmaster (known as "Pa" Bruce) had written to all the parents, explaining why the mission was keeping the school open: "The British authorities have agreed to treat the school as a unit, without discrimination of nationality... we realise the impossibility of moving as a unit to any one of the home countries." He finished by asking for special prayer for the school "during these difficult days".

Almost all the children stayed at Chefoo for Christmas that year, including David, who had spent the previous Christmas in a missionary home in Kunming, en route to school. The staff made special efforts to ensure that all the children had a magical time, with gifts, a Christmas tree, carol singing, and a visit from Father Christmas. Most of all, they were taught the significance of Christmas: the birth of Jesus, the coming of the Prince of Peace. In that time of war, the importance of God's love and protection was seen all the more clearly.

## The signs of war

There were very few new pupils when the next school year began in January, and those were mostly day students from the local expatriate community, for travel was almost impossible. Throughout 1941 the Japanese began to tighten their hold on China; the war in Europe escalated, and the US, with the support of Holland and Britain, cut off oil shipments to Japan. The Japanese retaliated with devastating effect: on 7th December they bombed Pearl Harbor in Hawaii. The next morning, Japanese soldiers arrived at Chefoo School and arrested Pa Bruce.

Until then, the school had continued much as usual, but the knowledge that the head teacher was imprisoned swept fear throughout the little community. Even the youngest children realised that something bad and dangerous was happening, and prayers were said daily for his safety. Pa Bruce was interrogated for several weeks, and released late in January, looking thin and tired. He had convinced the Japanese that he was not a spy, but the army began to take a new interest in the school. A notice was posted by the gate, stating that the entire compound was the property of His Imperial Majesty the Emperor of Japan. Soldiers came and made an inventory of all school and personal property, and various buildings were requisitioned for army use. No one was allowed to leave the compound, and soldiers stood guard at the gate. It was clear that the presence of so many Europeans would not be tolerated for long. Efforts by the mission to arrange evacuation of the whole school were unsuccessful. Some parents who worked locally made arrangements for their children to join them, but others thought it better to leave the children where they were safe and cared for, rather than risk the dangers of travel at such a time. They had little idea of what was being planned for Chefoo School.

Meanwhile, the staff were using all their ingenuity to continue to run the school as usual.
With no mail allowed in or out, and hence no
money to pay Chinese staff, they arranged rotas
so that cleaning and table-laying was done by
teachers and older pupils. Rationing was in force,
so bread was carefully limited, and interesting
menus designed, in which tofu – Chinese bean
curd – featured largely. Clothing became hard to
buy, so they unravelled their own scarves and
knitwear and knitted cardigans for the children.
Then, in November 1942, the order came:
everyone in the school was to be interned at the
Presbyterian mission compound at Temple Hill.

If the adults were alarmed at this development,
they gave no sign to their charges. Their message
to the children was always the same: God is sov-
ereign over every circumstance. His good hand
will guide us and protect us and our loved ones,
whatever happens. One teacher, Stanley
Houghton, had written a special setting of Psalm
46: "God is our refuge and strength, an ever-
present help in trouble. Therefore we will not
fear". It became the theme tune of the school,

and they sang it as they marched the two miles inland to their first camp. David was nine years old: he had spent a third of his life at boarding-school. War had prevented him from returning home to his parents and the baby brother he had never seen, and now he was being ejected from the security of his school "home" too. He could so easily have grown into a timid, insecure child during those years, institutionalised and unsure of his own self-worth and identity. Yet he recalls marching cheerfully up the hill with his friends, singing the psalm with confidence and under-standing. School life – the only life he knew – was built on trust in God. Parents might be shad-owy figures, far away in his memory, but his teachers encouraged him to pray for them, and he knew they were praying for him. Somehow, in prayer, they were all held together in the love of God. One day, they would be a family again.

Meanwhile, his teachers, too, were leaving their home – home, for some of them, for over thirty years. Yet they told their pupils that they could leave it cheerfully: the children were more important than the school, and community was more important than buildings. They could love and care for each other in any place. And each and every one of them was precious to God, who would love and care for them in every place and time. It was a set of values which would go with the children throughout their lives.

## Temple Hill

The girls' school was placed in a house about half a mile away from Temple Hill; the rest of the school was allocated three Western-style houses, each of which had eight rooms. Into the first house they crammed the 72 children and adults of the prep school; the second held the 58 pupils and staff of the boys' school; the third was for the older missionaries, who had retired in China and were attached to the school, together with a few of the older boys, to help with the work of the house – comparative luxury, with only 45 people in eight rooms!

Conditions were poor: the limited sanitation consisted of open outdoor toilets, and water for washing and cooking was in short supply, carried from a distant pump. One problem at least had been foreseen by experienced teachers of small children: before leaving the school, each child had been told to take the enamel potty from under his bed. Those potties travelled with the children throughout their years of internment, together with the poor bundle of bedding and personal belongings they were allowed. David was mortified by being encumbered with this embarrassing article, but he had one other prized possession: his battered box of dominoes, the precious gift from his parents three years earlier.

At first, the school was expected to buy all its own food, though later the Japanese agreed to send in some rations – even so, catering was a nightmare, cooking on primitive wood-burning stoves. Many of the children had already lost weight, though malnutrition had so far been avoided with the help of daily doses of cod-liver oil. Mrs Lack and Mrs Martin, wife of the Latin teacher Gordon Martin, embarked on a programme of mixed farming to supplement their diet. As well as growing vegetables in a plot in the compound, they bought two piglets, which they proceeded to fatten on meagre scraps and potato peelings, and some chickens and geese for eggs. Help came from other quarters, too: Rudolph Arendt was a member of the Liebenzeller Mission, an associate of CIM (China Inland Mission), and as a German national he was not interned. He used his freedom to smuggle mail and food into the camp, dumping bags of rice over the compound wall at night, and even managing to bring in a goat to provide milk.

The pupils were unaware of all these concerns. They were enjoying a dramatic adventure which still seemed more like a long camping trip than a disaster. Bedding had to be distributed over the floor of every room and up in the attics each night, and cleared away each day to make room to work and eat. Even though they had to take their share of the chores, peeling potatoes or washing dishes, school routine went on. Lessons continued as usual among the cabin trunks and boxes ranged around the walls of each room.

Each house had a single stove but coal was in short supply, so the coal dust was swept up, gathered together and mixed with clay to make coal balls, which would burn sullenly and give out a little heat. Most of the children suffered from chilblains that winter. Life became easier in the summer, when it was usually warm enough to take bedding outside and sleep under the stars, a relief from the cramped bedrooms.

Nevertheless, they were still sheltered from the reality of the war: conditions were far worse for many of the Chinese outside the camp, who were close to starvation. Inside the compound, the teachers resolutely kept up their spirits with concerts and comic songs, and even a newspaper, the *Temple Hill Tatler*. Evelyn Davey, the much loved teacher of the eight- and nine-year-olds, wrote of the early days in the camp: "It was all friendly and picnic-like, and only the presence of the Japanese soldiers, complete with bayonets, reminded us that we really were being interned in enemy territory." She always preserved her sense of fun. On the day they marched out of Chefoo School for Temple Hill, she had her basket over her arm. One of the small children saw a tiny paw appear over the edge. The whisper went around, "Miss Davey's smuggled out her cat!" With a mischievous wink at the children Miss Davey tucked away the paw and walked demurely past the guards, who noticed nothing.

In September 1943 came unwelcome news: all foreigners from Peking (Beijing), Tientsin (Tianjing), Tsingtao (Qingdao) and Chefoo would be interned together at Weihsien. This meant travelling by boat from Chefoo to Tsingtao and then a further journey by train. Everything had to be packed up again, and the school marched back along the long road to Chefoo.

On the morning of departure, Ailsa Carr, the prep school principal, gathered her pupils together and read them Psalm 93: "The Lord reigns." "God is our King," she told them. "We do not have to be afraid, because he is in control." The children looked up at her trustingly: all the adults in their young lives showed this same faith in God, and it underpinned their view of a world which could so easily have seemed threatening and filled with danger. Miss Carr embodied her favourite Bible verse: "Let the beloved of the Lord rest secure in him, for he shields him all day long" (Deuteronomy 33:12).

The boat provided by the Japanese for their journey was an alarming sight: rusty, battered and desperately overcrowded. Two hundred children and staff were packed into the hold, which was battened down at night, with no one allowed on deck. The energetic Miss Davey noted in her diary, "Two long, wooden shelves ran the length of the hold, and the children were packed top to tail, like sardines. There were no toilet facilities!" She congratulated herself on the foresight which had insisted on the enamel potties: the journey took two days and two nights, and many of the children were seasick.

The railway journey which followed took seven hours, and on arrival at Weihsien station they were given two minutes to leave the train. Much of the luggage had already been lost or looted; more was left on board in the scramble to disembark. Trucks transported them to yet another Presbyterian mission compound which had been seized by the Japanese. The wooden gates bore an inscription in Chinese: "The Courtyard of the Happy Way". They had arrived at Weihsien Concentration Camp.

# Weihsien

When it was owned by the American mission, the compound had included a school, seminary, hospital and several homes. Now the houses had been taken by the Japanese for their quarters, and the 1,500 internees were to be housed in some ramshackle, low huts and two high dormitory buildings. Food was prepared in three large public kitchens; the hospital had been dismantled, and there were only primitive latrines and open cesspools for sanitation. The camp at Temple Hill began to look pleasant by comparison.

In fact, on the whole the civilian concentration camps were better places than the military ones: the internees were given a great deal of freedom to organise their own affairs. Weihsien managed itself admirably: the largest group of inmates were from the missionary communities, and there was a general spirit of cheerful co-operation.

Everyone had work to do: the adults organised rotas for kitchen duties, cleaning and laundry, and the children pumped and carried water for washing. They gathered wood and scavenged in the ash heaps for unburned coal and charcoal for the stoves, and constructed home-made candles. David and his friends specialised in large four-wick candles, which could be used for frying old bread crusts or mushrooms in peanut oil, a special treat.

Food was a continual preoccupation. A typical menu consisted of two slices of bread for breakfast, with some porridge made from millet or sorghum; lunch was stew made from mushy egg-plant, known as SOS (Same Old Stew), and supper was soup – usually a watered-down version of SOS. Occasional Red Cross parcels were allowed in, which supplemented their diet with unexpected treats: butter, powdered milk, Spam and chocolate. Most of the time, however, there was no milk or cheese to provide calcium for growing bones, so Evelyn Davey took to collecting the shells from black-market eggs, grinding them to powder, and feeding each child with a spoonful each day.

The eggs were provided by the ingenuity and daring of a group of Roman Catholic priests, whose room was close to the perimeter wall, an excellent position for contact with Mrs Kang, the supplier. At night, Mrs Kang would funnel eggs through a drainage tunnel under the wall, where they would be collected by Father Scanlon. One night he was caught by the guards and sentenced to fifteen days' solitary confinement, a severe punishment for most people. The camp was highly amused: Father Scanlon was a Trappist monk, whose vow of silence had been forcibly interrupted by his internment. Solitary confinement was unlikely to worry him!

Clothing was also a problem: everyone's clothing wore out, but the children were growing out of their clothes, too, and a complicated system of hand-me-downs was operated by the teachers. In the summer, the boys wore only shorts, and they went barefoot almost all year round. Curtains, blankets and mattress covers were cut up and made into trousers and shirts, and tablecloths made into underwear – sometimes with startling patterns. Everything ended up a uniform shade of grey, however, since there was very little soap available, and although washing was done regularly the laundry was never really clean.

Diseases such as malaria, dysentry, hepatitis and typhoid were all endemic in the camp. With malnutrition compromising everyone's immune system, it required heroic efforts to keep the children healthy. Yet with over 1,500 people in the camp, there were only 28 deaths in two years.

## In speech and action

Whatever their own fears and concerns, the teachers of Chefoo School continued to fulfil faithfully the charge they had been given to care for their pupils. They taught the children about their faith, but their actions demonstrated it even more eloquently. They tried to make life as normal as possible for them in very abnormal circumstances, and their serenity, confidence and courage reassured the children that they were held safely in the hand of God, even in the midst of deprivation and danger.

Life went on all around them: there were two weddings among the Chefoo staff, and they contrived to celebrate the occasions with wedding cake made from a variety of unexpected ingredients. Babies were born in camp, their coming celebrated with joy, and there were also deaths. The Japanese did their best to block the black market trading with the Chinese living outside the camp, and when a Chinese man was electrocuted on the live wire which ran around the compound's outer fence, his body was left hanging on the wire as a warning to others. Such sights were traumatic for the young people inside the camp.

Death came especially close when Brian Thompson, son of one of the mission doctors, was also electrocuted. As they gathered for evening roll-call, some of the boys were playfully leaping up to touch a wire across the courtyard, but Brian was taller than the others, and caught hold of it with one hand. He fell to the damp ground, bringing the wire with him, and all efforts to resuscitate him failed. Pa Bruce had to conduct a funeral service for one of his own pupils.

Every child there had just had a lesson in the precariousness of life. They had seen someone their own age die in front of their eyes. How could Pa Bruce reassure them of the love of God?

He told them that though Brian had missed the roll-call in the camp, he had answered the roll-call in heaven; God, who numbers the stars, knew Brian by name, and had a place prepared for him. The children knew that not only did they have the physical security of the care of their teachers, but they also had the spiritual security of the love of God.

There was another hero for the boys in the warden of their roll-call area: he was Eric Liddell. Eric was famous as the athlete who had refused to run on a Sunday in the 1924 Olympics, but had later won the gold medal and set a world record in the 400-metre race. His story was immortalised in the film *Chariots of Fire*, but little attention was paid to the fact that he subsequently went to China with the London Missionary Society, and was interned in March 1943, along with other enemy nationals, and sent to Weihsien Concentration Camp.

Eric carried his Olympic achievements lightly; he was head of the recreation committee, and managed to organise athletics events and sports days for the whole camp. He even umpired the small boys' barefoot soccer games: the children knew him as Uncle Eric. He also supported the school by teaching science to the older students, but he always had time to befriend people. He put up a shelf for a Russian prostitute in the camp, who said that he was the only man who did something for her without wanting any return. His special gift was in talking to young people, especially the older teenagers, who were frustrated by the way their young lives had been brought to a halt by the war. They were impatient to finish their education, to find a career, to marry and get on with normal life. Eric would spend many hours walking and talking with them, listening to their hopes and fears, and turning their questions and longing for freedom gently towards faith in God.

Here was a man who accepted his circumstances with patience. He must have missed his wife and daughters, and the third little girl, born in Canada, whom he had never seen. Yet he continued faithfully to do the work he knew God had given him. By early 1945 the privations of captivity were affecting everyone, and Eric had slowed down a little; he suffered from frequent headaches. One cold day in February, David saw Uncle Eric walking slowly around the yard where he had taught the boys to play basketball and rounders. That night, he died of a brain tumour.

The children of Chefoo School formed part of the guard of honour at his funeral. Once again they saw death close up, but it held no terrors for them, because they knew it had held no fears for the man who had died, confident in the love of Jesus and the joy that awaited him. Eric Liddell was their hero, not just because he was an Olympic medallist, but because they saw in him a man who was totally committed to putting God first, and who lived his life for God in service to others.

## From the land of the enemy

By this time the war was almost over. Although 15th August 1945 was VJ Day ("Victory in Japan"), there was no change in camp routine. Whatever the Japanese knew about these developments, they gave no sign to their captives. Then, two days later, there was a drone overhead, and an American B24 plane flew low over the camp. Everyone, children and adults alike, ran outside to watch it pass, fearing that the Japanese would open fire. To everyone's disappointment it banked and turned away, but left behind it an amazing trail: seven parachutes floated gently down towards the camp.

The guards made no attempt to stop them as the internees ran to the gates and wrenched them open, running outside down the track to meet the seven GIs who were disentangling themselves from their canopies. Cheering and waving, they hoisted the soldiers onto their shoulders and carried them into camp; not a shot was fired. The commandant and his officers surrendered immediately.

One of the Americans strode into camp and said, "Take me to Mr Bruce!" He was Lieutenant Jimmy Moore of the US Navy, and a graduate of Chefoo School himself. He had volunteered for this dangerous mission (for no one knew what desperate steps the Japanese might take in defeat) because he knew that so many of the internees were missionaries and children from his old school.

It took some time to arrange for the liberation

of the camp, so the Americans dropped bundles of supplies to improve conditions in the short term: clothing, medicines, toiletries and food. For David and his friends, used to a near-starvation diet, the boxes brought unimaginable delights. They had long forgotten the taste of chocolate or tinned fruit, but ketchup was entirely new: David thought it was a very thick, sweet drink, until its purpose was explained. And he was mystified by chewing-gum, which he swallowed whole.

Meanwhile, the adults were hearing the terrible truth about the ending of the war and the dropping of the atom bomb. It was a sombre note among all their rejoicing.

It was the end of September before the prisoners were released – first to Tsingao and then on to Hong Kong. The children were amazed by their first contacts with the outside world – money, shops, running water, proper toilets. They were treated to picnics and outings by the Red Cross, and gradually the truth dawned on them: at last, they were free. For many of them, this was simply another change of surroundings.

They could hardly take in the fact that they would soon be going home, because home had scarcely any meaning for them. School had been their home – then Temple Hill and then Weihsien. Family was only a dim memory for the younger ones; the people who loved them were their teachers and their friends.

The Japanese invasion of China had overtaken many missionary families, and parents had been forced out of the country, leaving their children behind in camps. Parts of China were suffering from a four-way conflict, as battles raged internally between government troops and the Communist Red Army, as well as with the Japanese and local bandits or guerrilla groups. David Michell's parents, with his younger sister and brother, had to leave their home in Kunming and make their way home to Australia without him.

Another missionary mother told how hard it was to bear the separation, and leave the country knowing that her children were prisoners of war. Two Canadians, Edith and John Bell, were working in northern China when they heard a rumour that the Japanese had killed all the prisoners in Weihsien camp. Edith was terrified, but she held fast to her faith in God's promises. Her special verses were Jeremiah 31:16,17:

> "Restrain your voice from weeping and your eyes from tears, for your work will be rewarded," declares the Lord. "They will return from the land of the enemy... Your children will return to their own land."

In January 1946 Edith and John made their way home — a long and arduous journey by troopship. They knew that some prisoners of war had already been released, but had no idea where their own three children were. When they docked in New York they were handed a letter from the mission, telling them that their children had arrived home two days before, and were already in Toronto, waiting for them. Edith could scarcely believe it. God's promise was fulfilled: her children were delivered, not only "from the land of the enemy", but they had also returned to their own land, as Jeremiah had said.

David and his sister Joyce travelled home to Sydney on a converted aircraft carrier, HMS

Reaper, with other Australian teachers and pupils. It was a momentous trip for David, marking the beginning of a new life and the end of an old one. The new life was signalled by two things: he saw his first ever film, *Meet me in St Louis* – a dazzling introduction to the Western way of life – and he was given a free Gideon Bible. In this he signed his name, to register his commitment to Christ as Lord of his life. Even at the age of twelve, he had some understanding of what the war years had entailed, and he knew how much suffering he had been spared by the grace of God. The end of that old life of hunger and poverty he celebrated by throwing overboard two possessions he had carried throughout the war: the hated potty from Chefoo School, and the chipped enamel pie dish from which he had eaten his meagre meals. Then he turned to face the coast of a country he had never visited, to meet the parents he had not seen for half his life.

## Children of God

Walter Michell, David's father, couldn't wait for his children to disembark. As soon as the ship had berthed at the wharf in Sydney and the gang-plank was lowered, he sprinted up it to the flight deck, where they stood peering out over the rail. Joyce threw herself into his arms, and he reached out and gathered David to him, too. All David's hesitancy left him, together with his fears that he wouldn't recognise his father. His mother waited below with Joan and four-year-old Brian, whom the other children had never seen. They were a family, together again at last.

Other families around the world were rejoicing to have their children restored to them. Alice Taylor recorded that her four children emerged from Weihsien camp with no emotional problems and in excellent health. When they went back to school in the United States, they were two years ahead of students their own age. They had lived through the war, separated from their parents, suffering poor food and living conditions, exposed to brutality and death and danger. Any child might have been damaged, scarred and depressed by such experiences. Yet these children emerged healthy, balanced, secure in the love of

God and equipped with a faith that would last their lifetime.

David Michell went on to teach in Australia, and then became an OMF missionary in Japan for ten years. He settled in Toronto and became the National Director of OMF for Canada. He attributes his safe passage through those terrible times to the faith, love and care of the real war heroes: the teachers of Chefoo School.

# The Day the
# Earth Shook

In Taiwan, they call it "Nine two one" – the fateful morning of 21st September 1999 (09.21.99) when the earthquake struck, and life for many people was never the same again.

Earthquakes are nothing new in Taiwan. The island off the coast of mainland China is scored by more than 50 fault lines, and minor tremors occur all the time. There are over 15,000 of these each year, mostly too small to be felt by anything other than extremely sensitive seismic equipment, designed to register every tiny movement of the earth. Even the larger earthquakes are usually brief: if you are standing up, walking, or even driving your car, you probably won't notice them; if you are sitting down or lying in bed, you might be aware of the movement. The Taiwanese people are stoical about their shifting island.

But 921 was different. It caused the deaths of 2,000 people, and made 100,000 homeless. It registered 7.6 on the Richter scale, and caused massive damage: buildings toppled, walls collapsed, and roads were torn up. Even more impressive to the Christians working in Taiwan was the effect it had on people's lives, as it disturbed their comfortable lifestyles and shook up their assumptions about security, about Christianity, and about God.

## Earthquake!

In Taichung, Angela and Martin Symonds were asleep in their apartment on the eleventh floor of a fourteen-storey building. At 1.47 a.m. they were woken by a loud creaking and groaning; their bedroom swayed and rocked, and books and ornaments crashed from the shelves.

"What's going on?" said Martin, sleepily. Then they both exclaimed together: "Earthquake!"

Their bed shifted under them as they threw back the covers and staggered towards the doorway: under the doorframe is the safest place in the room. As the first shock subsided, they threw on shorts and T-shirts and grabbed the first coats and shoes they could find, groping in the darkness – none of the lights was working. Martin pushed aside a heap of fallen books and pulled open the front door, and saw with relief that the emergency lighting in the hall was on. Families were emerging from all the other flats, and hurrying down the dimly lit stairways. There was only one thought in everyone's mind: to get out of the building in case it collapsed.

Angela is a University Christian Fellowship staff worker, and on her way downstairs she stopped to check on Christine, one of the language students who lived on the fourth floor: her apartment was empty. Outside, the dark street was full of families hurrying away, trying to find open ground where there was less danger of collapsing buildings. Every few minutes there were further shocks, and people clung together, trying to stay upright; cracks appeared in the roads.

Martin and Angela found Christine outside in the road, and together they walked to the home of another missionary family they knew. They found them and their two small children standing at the corner of their street, along with all their neighbours. Some people had switched on their car headlights, to give some light, and others had tuned in their car radios, to pick up any news. That was how Martin and Angela discovered that the centre of the earthquake was at Puli, about 35km to the south. There, presumably, the effects would be even greater.

As the aftershocks grew fewer, people began to settle down to wait for the dawn, mostly huddled in groups in open areas or sleeping in their cars. Martin, Angela and Christine tried to sleep in a car with another student, but it was impossible to rest: the night was chilly, and everyone was nervous and edgy, alert to every sound and waiting for another tremor.

When it began to get light at about 6 a.m., they climbed back up the eleven floors to view the extent of the damage. There were no visible cracks in the walls, but two bookcases were broken. Every book had been shaken off the shelves, and things were strewn across the floor; a few glass jars had shattered, but the china cupboard was still closed and everything inside was intact. To their surprise, the telephone was still working, and, after conferring with friends, they decided that the prayer meeting scheduled for that afternoon should go ahead as normal. The topic for the day, planned weeks in advance, was "Preparation for Crises".

Across the city, Andy and Mei-ling Wilson had a similar experience. They lived in a densely-populated housing complex of some 4,500 apartments, in buildings up to 24 storeys high. Mei-ling was born in Taiwan, and is accustomed to earthquakes: she knew at once that this was "the big one". They too joined the mass exodus as terrified people fled from the built-up areas, fearing falling masonry and toppling buildings. Many of their church members lived close by, and they met up with several friends, holding hands and praying together as the ground shook and buckled beneath their feet. At that moment they appreciated the difference made by their faith in God: praying seemed to spread peace and calm among their little group of believers.

Their building sustained greater damage, so, apart from returning briefly to collect a few essentials, they had to move out until it was inspected and declared safe. They took shelter with some friends on the campus of Tunghai University, staying in their small bungalow – a safer option, as it was possible to run outside quickly when an aftershock struck. Another friend at the university opened up the biology laboratories to provide shelter for some of the families, so that there was room for the children to lie down and sleep. Many people, however, preferred to stay outside. They sat in small groups throughout the night, chatting and making lists of what they would rescue from their homes, if they were able to get back into them. As Mei-ling said, "It made everyone start to think about what was most important to them."

Such stories were repeated across the island. In Tung Shih, a city on the coast 100 km south of Puli, Max and Waltraud Graf were thrown out of bed by the first shock. Furniture crashed around their room, blocking the doorway and making escape impossible; they knelt and prayed, "Lord Jesus, help us!" as the house trembled around them. When they managed to clear their doorway, they got in the car and drove out of the stricken city to safety. Almost every street had fallen buildings. James Lyou, a Christian actor, had been asleep on the seventh floor of a high-rise block. Five floors below him were crushed, and he walked out unharmed from what was now the second floor.

Taipei, the capital of Taiwan, is some 145km north of Puli. The earthquake was so violent that its effects were felt there, too, and many people in the city thought that they were at the epicentre itself. Two high-rise buildings fell, including the twelve-storey Sungshan Hotel, which crushed its first eight floors: 50 people were trapped in the rubble and thirteen died. One man described walking across a room as being like swimming in the sea – you were pushed and pulled by invisible currents. Others spoke of the terrifying noises of creaking and cracking in the swaying buildings, made more frightening by the total darkness of the city when the electricity failed; the moon and stars were blotted out by rain clouds in Taipei that night.

In Puli itself, there was devastation. Buildings peeled apart, their walls stripped away like open-fronted doll's houses. The ground split open, bridges fell and roads tipped up at acute angles. One hospital was completely destroyed. At the other, Puli Christian Hospital, its Director, David Wong, had just pulled up outside after a four-hour drive from Taipei. Suddenly his van was tossed up and down, and a tree split and fell just in front of him, crashing through the roof of a parked car. As soon as the first tremor passed, David got out and ran into the hospital to start organising the emergency work which he knew would be needed. Triage units were set up outside to minister to the 700 injured who soon began to arrive; these included a six-year-old boy with an amputated leg, the sole survivor of a family of six. At one time, 72 bodies were piled into refrigerated containers usually used for transporting food. It was to be almost three weeks before David was able to return to his home in Taichung.

## Rescue

As day dawned over Taiwan, people everywhere were trying to recover from the initial shock and come to terms with the damage. A number of power stations were out of action, and dams had broken, so both electricity and water supplies were interrupted. The army began to distribute emergency supplies of clean water and medicines, to prevent epidemics of cholera and dysentery.

The government took over an athletics stadium in the central town of Nantou, and soon uniformed soldiers, civilian volunteers and local charitable organisations were filling it. The same scene was repeated in other cities: in Taichung, helicopters landed on the university sports field, and ambulances ferried the injured from there to hospital. In many places, the country roads were impassable. The first priority was rescue, and the army was supported by international rescue teams, who flew in at once, the Japanese bringing special expertise gained from their recent experiences in the earthquake at Kobe. Members of the OMF international team were able to interpret for the German and Swiss rescuers as they brought bodies out of the rubble.

To the Taiwanese, death is a curse; if there is a death in the family, members will avoid visiting friends for fear of carrying the curse into their homes. As a result, it is usual for immediate family members to look after the dead and prepare their bodies alone. They were amazed and touched by the willingness of the Christians to help them – not only to comfort them in their grief, but to dig in the rubble and lift out the bodies of their loved ones, to handle them and to care for them. This active care reached more hearts than any sermon could have done, and spoke volumes about the love that the Christians had for them and their confidence in the face of death.

Strict anti-earthquake building regulations have been in place in Taiwan since 1972, so most of the newer buildings were designed to withstand the shock. A system of inspection was set up immediately after the earthquake, to reassure people who wished to know if it was safe to move back into their homes, and it found that many buildings had sustained only minor cracks. Some fell, however, including three high-rise buildings in Yunlin county; they had all been built by the same construction company, who had used empty plastic bottles and tin cans as filler, to save on concrete. Tent cities sprang up on every playing field and open space, as people decided that they were safer outside in the open.

There was much to be thankful for: if the earthquake had happened during the day, casualties would have been far greater. All 137 schools in the area around Taichung were ruined; during the day, thousands of schoolchildren would have been trapped. Much of the housing in the city has three storeys, built on supports, with the ground floor open for car parking. Many of these supports shifted and fell, so that the upper floors came down intact, but crushed the parked cars. Most of the inhabitants, sleeping upstairs, were safe; during the day they would have been down in the street, shopping or talking with neighbours.

Out in the villages it was a different story. Rural homes are often built of mud and straw, and they had crumbled to dust, leaving the people with nothing. The central mountain region of the island was the hardest hit, and many villages were cut off entirely.

The OMF missionaries in Taiwan were suffering the same shock and trauma as everyone else, but they gathered together to pray and assess the situation. The first need seemed to be to transport supplies of food, clothing and medicines out to the villages, so those who had cars available began to make journeys into the surrounding countryside. This was not without its dangers: Andy Wilson reported travelling into the mountains to reach an isolated village, and having to drive off the road four times, each time taking to a dry river-bed; on the way back that night he found the road blocked by a boulder the size of a car, brought down by one of the many aftershocks. The following day a twelve-storey apartment block fell right across the same road. Another team was cut off completely by aftershocks, and had to be brought out by helicopter.

In the years leading up to the millennium, the churches had began a Year 2000 Gospel Movement, with the aim of building up the churches and the Christians in Taiwan and adding to their number. It had successfully linked together churches of various denominations, and set up the Chinese Christian Relief Association. This organisation now came into its own: it set up central points for collecting relief supplies, and arranged for these to be taken to the most needy areas. There was a great deal of willingness to help, but there was no one in charge: Mei-ling set about bringing order out of chaos, and with the help of friends she arranged some co-ordination to make sure that people knew where to go and what to take with them. She felt that it was an excellent witness. The Taiwanese often ask why there are so many denominations among the Christians: now they could see them all working together in harmony. "In twenty years as a Christian," said Mei-ling, "I have never seen Christians working together like this."

## A vision for the church

Three days after the earthquake was the date for the Taiwanese Mid-autumn Festival, traditionally a time when families get together for celebration. Instead, many families were homeless or bereaved. The president declared three days of mourning for the dead, with all flags flying at half-mast. Some feasting went on, though – with electricity available only sporadically, all the food in the freezers would soon go off, so people prepared large meals to use it up. Restaurants managed to open in spite of the power shortages, using candles for lighting and bottled gas for cooking. There was a spirit of determination to get on with clearing up and resume normal life, but this was hard for many people who were still suffering from shock and grief.

David Eastwood drove a van to Ming Chien in Nantou County, one of the worst-affected areas, to set up a relief centre. He and his colleagues found that supplies of food and clothing were readily available, but people were glad to receive radios and mosquito repellant. He spent the evening among the tents in the school grounds, drinking tea and talking to the people there. The few whose homes were intact were unwilling to return to them, in case of further earthquakes. Everyone had a story to tell – of narrow escapes, or how they managed to find and contact friends and family, or how they found their neighbours dead – everyone needed to talk.

David was impressed by the beauty of the area: on all sides, tall mountains reached up into the mist, while the plateau was filled with neat tea plantations and pineapple fields. Yet he felt it was a place of spiritual darkness. Only ninety small churches are dotted around an area with a population of half a million. In all the tiny villages there were people like those he had already met, desperate to talk about their terrifying experiences and make sense of what had happened to them. How were they ever going to have the chance to hear about the real peace that only Jesus could give them? Even in the midst of the destruction, most people seemed to have few material needs, but they were pleased to talk. Most of all, they were moved that someone should care enough to come and find out how they were, especially since the Christians had come from the relative safety of the city in the east, out to the more active and dangerous mountain areas.

In Ping Ding village, he unpacked and sorted the medicines they had brought with them; this convinced the local people that he must be a doctor, so he found himself dressing cuts and grazes and looking at more serious injuries – the doctors who arrived the next day were definitely an answer to prayer. Meanwhile, their activities had become a focus of interest for many of the children, who were wandering around with nothing to do. David and his colleagues borrowed tables and chairs from a kindergarten, and produced colouring books with pictures of Bible stories. Soon the children were colouring happily while they talked about the story of Jesus, while a tape of children's songs played in the background. In one of these, the singers shouted "Jesus loves me!" and, as he heard the children singing along, David thought how wonderful it would be if they really knew it was true. Many of the children had lost relatives in the earthquake; they were unsettled by their new life camping out in tents, and most had trouble sleeping at night. Their fears had not diminished since the night of the quake, because the aftershocks which occurred every day were a constant reminder. The team taught the children to sing "I've got peace like a river", and told them about a God who loves them and can help them when they are afraid. One woman said, "This is the first time since the earthquake that I've seen my children smile."

They also gave away books of Christian testimonies to the adults who came to see what was going on, and one man took away a Bible. In between, they worked to restore order to the kindergarten and council office: the building was structurally undamaged, but the mess of broken furniture, smashed glass and fallen books needed clearing up. The fridge and freezer were full of food which had been rotting for nearly a week.

This trip encouraged David's vision for the work of the church in Taiwan. It was a sign of maturity that all the churches had been able to work together so effectively, bringing supplies and practical help to the rural areas. Yet most of the churches were based in the cities. Would the disaster result in city pastors being willing to work in the villages, and their congregations being willing to come and spread the gospel in these places? There would be work to do for a long time to come – not only houses to be rebuilt but lives too, as people sought release from the fear and nightmares that surrounded them. How would they hear the good news of Jesus unless the church was willing to work among them?

## The building of barns

Back in the city, Andy and Mei-ling were getting to know their neighbours. In an area of high-density housing, it simply wasn't possible to know all the people who lived in the same building as you, let alone those in adjacent buildings. Now everyone was spread out – in tents, in the buildings on the university campus, or sleeping in their cars on the streets. The Taiwanese are a private people, focusing on their close family ties, and unwilling to look for contacts outside their family circles. Yet it seemed that a new sense of community was developing, and people were more willing to talk to each other. In the tent cities, activities sprang up: someone was offering hairdressing services; a cookery class was started, to help people cope with the primitive cooking facilities available; an English class began to meet. And always there was this need to talk.

One very common anxiety was about money. In a highly materialist society, property was important: the earthquake had destroyed thousands of homes overnight. Where people owned their own home they had lost their property; where they had mortgages, they had lost their home but still had a huge debt to pay off. One man ran a business building houses for sale: every house on his building site was demolished, which meant financial ruin for him and his family. Even the houses left standing presented problems: whether they suffered severe structural damage or minor plaster cracks, everything needed repair, and repairs cost money. House values dropped, and the government brought in a system of low-interest loans.

Many of their neighbours congratulated Andy and Mei-ling because they had only rented, and not bought their flat; then they confided their financial concerns. People who at first had been rejoicing that they had escaped with their lives were now counting the cost of the earthquake and realising that they had serious financial problems. The suicide rate went up. It was clear that once the immediate material needs had been met, people would still have psychological, emotional and spiritual problems – problems which new building programmes would not solve.

Andy and Mei-ling lived simply compared to their neighbours: they owned very little, so they had little to lose. Andy e-mailed home on the day after the earthquake: "Our known personal financial losses mount up to 20p (a drinking glass that fell to the floor)!" Yet they had great sympathy for their neighbours who were going through another stage of trauma. They noticed a change in their mind-set: people had begun to realise that they could not control their lives or plan for the future with any certainty. They all knew people like the rich man in Luke's Gospel, who planned to tear down his barns and build bigger ones to store his grain and his goods, and to whom God said, "You fool! This very night your life will be demanded from you." When their neighbours died, when one building stood and another fell, where could they find security? Mei-ling said, "People would say 'I am a Buddhist' or 'I believe in God', but what they actually believed in was themselves. Now God is shaking up all their assumptions." She and Andy found wonderful opportunities to share the gospel.

## Rebuilding lives

Several weeks after the earthquake, David Eastwood made another trip to the mountain villages. This time he found that the cracked and broken roads had already been repaired, and much of the rubble of fallen houses had been removed. There were still many tents in use, some of them outside houses which looked sound, as though people were still afraid to move back inside. One family moved indoors only when the weather became really cold, and even then the children refused to sleep upstairs, preferring to curl up near the front door, in case they had to leave in a hurry.

In Chi-chi, a town right at the epicentre of the earthquake, two sites of temporary housing had been donated by a Buddhist relief agency in Japan. The homes were made of metal, wood and plastic, and contained new beds, cookers and a framed Buddhist text. These were a great improvement on tents, and people were moving their few belongings inside. A generous gift from a church in Hong Kong had allowed the team to bring evangelistic material and also boxes of fruit: it is customary in Taiwanese society to bring a small gift, such as fruit, when visiting. David and his team began to call at these homes, but they succeeded in meeting only three families in two hours, because each time they were invited inside to talk.

They were welcomed at every home, and everyone was happy to receive prayer; one old lady said she wanted the Christian God to give her peace. Even the two team members who stayed at their base had been visited by people asking if someone would pray with them, as they were afraid and unable to sleep at night. That evening, a cable TV station was making a live broadcast at the housing site, so the team of missionaries went along to watch. The interviewer, seeing foreigners in the crowd, approached David and asked why they were there. David told the cameras and the crowd that they knew people were afraid, and had come to pray for them – and with them – that God would give them peace in their hearts. The interviewer promptly moved on! However, someone else in the crowd came up to the microphone, and, instead of asking a question of the panel of local politicians, made a short speech. He said that on behalf of the local people he wished to thank the Christians for all the care and help they had given since the earthquake. At this there was a spontaneous burst of applause. Once again, the team realised how deeply felt was the need for love and listening, and for peace and reassurance.

The next day an old man took them to visit his relatives, Mr and Mrs Yang, living in a warehouse in the countryside. The old couple and a friend sat with David, drinking tea and talking; Mrs Yang was worried about her arm, which had been badly injured when she was trapped in the rubble of her house. All of them were suffering from shock and sleeping badly. The conversation turned from the earthquake to their fears, and how Jesus gives peace, and David spent two hours sharing the gospel and his own testimony, and praying with them. As they were leaving, the Yangs asked if he would lay hands on Mrs Yang and pray with her. It was an unusual request, but he complied. He felt God prompting him to invite them to repeat his words one sentence at a time, so they prayed together that God would help them to come to know him and his Son Jesus Christ and so have peace in their hearts. The Yangs invited him to return that evening and teach them some Christian songs.

That evening, David took with him an elderly couple from the church in Kaohsiung, and found that the Yangs' friend, Mr Liu, had also brought his wife to meet them. Mrs Yang told them that she had felt better all afternoon since they had prayed together; Mr Yang said that the pain in his leg had vanished. They sang songs together, and the elderly couple shared a powerful testimony. At the close of the evening, both the Yangs and the Lius prayed to receive Christ as their Saviour; they asked for Bibles, which the team promised to deliver the next day, but the two men insisted on returning to the centre with them and collecting their Bibles that night.

This story was repeated over and over again. As the team compared notes, they felt like spectators in a mighty work of the Holy Spirit, as he moved in people's hearts. All they had to do was to present the gospel simply and sincerely; everywhere, people's hearts were open to receive the message.

## The Spirit is moving

On the whole, Taiwan is affluent and successful; it is a society where materialism reigns. Large factories churn out consumer goods for the West, which are no less appreciated by consumers closer to home. Although many of the rural regions are still poor, the cities are full of the shops, offices and high-rise buildings that indicate a nation enjoying its prosperity. Yet as the buildings collapsed, as homes crumbled and treasured possessions were lost in the rubble, as even families and friends were missing, injured or dead, many people looked afresh on their priorities. Why strive for more money when the things it could buy could be lost in an instant? When the earth shook and the strongest walls had fallen, what had they searched for in the rubble? Not the television set or the motorcycle, but people – their loved ones, children and friends. When the dust was settling and the world was dark and silent, what had they longed for? Not the latest designer gadgets, but love, peace, and someone who would care enough to take time to listen to their deepest fears. Suddenly the missionaries who had lived among them for years acquired new importance. Even when they themselves were homeless, they cared enough to seek out those who had even less, and they listened and prayed with people who were shaken and shocked and bereaved.

All the missionaries on the island reported the same pattern: there was a new openness in people's hearts that far exceeded their expectations, and whole families were being converted. It was the same in rich areas and poor, in city, town and countryside. Now the churches are working together with renewed strength, and city churches are sending out teams to reach the isolated settlements. Workstations have been set up in the villages, and people go out at weekends to run medical and social work programmes, to provide a ministry of counselling, to run activities and clubs, and to provide opportunities to share the gospel.

The church in Taiwan is seeing a new out-pouring of love, and a willingness to reach out to its own people in evangelism. And the people are responding to the love of God with thankful hearts. This was the real earth-moving change that happened in Taiwan on 21st September.

# Dreaming
# Dreams

The Philippines consist of some 7,000 scraps of land in the South Pacific, of which around 700 islands are inhabited. The people are mainly Filipinos who speak Tagalog, the national language, and some English, as well as one of over 80 different dialects. They live in coastal towns and ports, and many still work on lowland farms or cut logs in the jungles. However, in the mountainous inland reaches of the islands live many tribal groups with unwritten languages, whose way of life has remained unchanged for centuries. Mindoro is one of the larger islands, and in its interior are hidden the people of six tribal groups, living an iron-age existence in scattered villages among the jungle.

Russell and Barbara Reed, a young American couple, were keen to work in Mindoro. Russell was pastor of a small church in Oregon, and Barbara was a teacher, but they were both committed to mission. In November 1953 they were waiting at the OMF language school in Singapore for their visas to the Philippines – and also expecting the birth of their first child. With the arrival of the paperwork came a terse message from the OMF office in Manila, doubtless from a harassed missionary who had spent weeks wrangling with the Filipino bureaucracy: "Get the Reeds to Manila as soon as possible. If that baby is born outside the Philippines it will need a visa, and that could take another nine months!"

So Barbara, eight-and-a-half months pregnant, squeezed herself uncomfortably into a small aircraft seat, and she and Russell flew north. Eleven days later, in a Manila hospital, their son Ricky was born. He was only three weeks old when they set off again for Mindoro, Barbara and Ricky travelling by air to the tiny airport at Calapan, and Russell and three other missionaries making the longer journey by ferry.

Barbara was met at the airport by Dr Jim Broomhall, OMF Field Superintendent for the Philippines, and a nephew of the great Hudson Taylor, founder of the China Inland Mission. Jim had arranged a *kalesa* – a small horse-drawn carriage with two big wheels – to take the mother and her tiny baby to the mission house in Calapan. Barbara was grateful for the canvas and plastic cover, which sheltered them from the winter monsoon wind and rain as they rattled through the streets. Her time in Singapore had prepared her for the tropical climate, the banana palms swaying in the wind, the evident poverty and the lack of sanitation. She felt only excitement that the adventure was about to begin – the adventure of bringing God's word to a people who walked in darkness.

The Mangyan – the tribal people of Mindoro – lived in isolated villages in the jungles and mountains, mostly far away from the lowland Filipinos. Their lives were not easy. When they did have contact with the lowlanders, they were often exploited by farmers who took their land and forced them to labour on it for minimal pay; they suffered the kind of discrimination that made them travel in the rear luggage section on buses, and their lack of education made them easy prey for cheats and swindlers. They were also oppressed by living in daily fear, not of human exploitation, but of the demons which they thought inhabited the rocks, trees and rivers of their island. They believed that these spirits could cause accidents, illness and death, so they sacrificed precious food to placate them, and watched superstitiously for signs of what the spirits wanted.

Barbara and Russell longed to reach these people with news of a loving God, who cared so much for them that he sent his Son to live in the world like them, to die for them and to open the way to eternal life. They dreamed of seeing the first believers come to faith, of building a church here as a beacon of light among the darkness of fear and oppression. They were especially delighted when Jim Broomhall told them where he wanted them to begin work – among the Tawbuid, a tribe of central Mindoro. There was only one problem: in a year on the island, no one from OMF had ever seen anyone from this tribe!

Barbara and Russell spent the next two years based at the National Agricultural School near the east coast of the island. Those years were eventful enough, what with learning languages, making friends, discovering how to buy and cook the local food, and caring for Ricky and a new baby, Becky. Barbara felt that she also spent the time learning to trust God and rely on his care for them. There was the night the Agricultural School was flooded, and they peered fearfully down between the slats of their floor to see the waters swirling below. What if the four-foot-high poles on which their house was built gave way? They had been so relieved when the rain stopped the next morning, and an old woman came splashing through the field with eggs, rice and bananas to sell for their meal. Then there was the time she had been washing clothes by the creek and had suddenly felt the need to check on Ricky. He had been sleeping peacefully when she left him, but she reached him just as he was turning blue, strangled by his cot harness. God had been caring for them – but they had still made no headway with their real work of reaching the Tawbuid tribes.

## First contact

Their next home was at Ligaya, near the coast of south-west Mindoro. A Filipino guide had told them there were some Tawbuid living near his farm in the foothills, so they made the transfer from the Agricultural School as soon as they could. Once they were settled, Russell and the guide trekked out to the farmhouse, and on the very first day they were rewarded. As they rounded a bend in the track, seven men emerged from the jungle. They wore only loincloths, with a knife hanging from a waist cord; their skin was a dusty clay colour, and one man was smoking a clay pipe. They stared at Russell in alarm, and the guide hurried to reassure them in Tagalog – they had never seen a white man before. Eventually, they agreed to take Russell and the guide to their home, where Russell painstakingly compiled a list of Tawbuid words, written phonetically, with their Tagalog and English translations. He handed his notes triumphantly to Barbara when he returned – they had finally begun their work!

This beginning led to further contacts. They found another small Tawbuid village, and gradually improved their grasp of their language. As the people became used to them, they were often allowed to stay for short periods in an empty house in the clearing. Barbara in particular gained a special friend, a Tawbuid woman who would come and sit with her as she watched Ricky and little Becky play around the house-poles with the other children, or prepared rice and sweet potatoes for their meal. They would laugh and joke together, and Barbara learned a great deal about the women's everyday life and their customs. All the people were friendly, and listened to what they had to say, and helped them when their language skills faltered. Yet no one seemed particularly responsive to their message.

Then tragedy struck: a pregnant woman of the tribe tripped and fell onto a jagged tree stump; it punctured her uterus, and her unborn baby died. Several days later, when Russell visited the village, he found it deserted. He searched the jungle on the other side of the fields and discovered the entire community making a new clearing and building new houses. Three more of their people had died, they said, from an illness which made breathing difficult – it sounded to Russell like pneumonia – and one of these was Barbara's friend. Clearly, the old village site was cursed, so they had to move away. While Russell was with them, another man developed the same symptoms and died. The Tawbuid had no access to medicines; they simply attributed every illness to the work of demons.

Now Barbara and Russell saw the real effects of those oppressive beliefs: the people sat huddled in their huts, and stuffed the cracks in the doorways and walls with leaves, to prevent evil spirits from entering and killing them, too. They were afraid to sleep at night, but kept a fire burning to ward off any lurking spirits which might be circling round the village. When another woman was dying, Russell visited her; she showed no symptoms except abject terror. She simply turned her face to the wall and died.

The Reeds were sick at heart: why were they such failures at preaching God's word? Here they were with a message that could literally save the lives of these people who were dying from fear and despair; they knew from experience that "perfect love casts out fear". Why were they unable to reach them?

It was at this low point that they received a

message from Jim Broomhall, asking them to visit eastern Mindoro, where two other missionaries had been working among the Tadyawan tribe around the Banus River. One missionary, Caroline Stickley, had reported that some Tawbuid tribesmen had begun to use the same river route for trading on the coast. They had been talking to the Tadyawan and expressed an interest in the message brought by the white people. They asked if there were any more of the white strangers, who spoke their language.

Barbara and Russell were confused. They had spent months searching for Tawbuid tribes when they were living near the east coast at the Agricultural School, but had never met even one. Now, after years of fruitless work on the other side of the island, they were being called back. If God really wanted them to reach the Tawbuid, why hadn't he led them there years ago? And why had they spent so much time working with the Tawbuid on the west coast, who clearly had no interest in their message? The only thing they had gained in all that time, it seemed, was a fluent grasp of the Tawbuid language.

## Led by the spirits

The Reeds made it a round trip, delivering the children to school in Manila for the new term, and then taking the ferry back to Mindoro and travelling down the east coast to talk to Caroline. Her story was exciting: one of her Tadyawan contacts, a man called Pedro, had met a Tawbuid called Tiban. Tiban's father had had a dream about some strangers who would come with some good teaching. All the Mangyan set great store by dreams, which they believed were sent by the spirits to guide them and foretell the future, so Tiban took the warning seriously. When he heard about the missionaries, he wanted to come and see them for himself. Pedro then added that many years ago, someone in the Tadyawan tribe had had a vision similar to that dream. He saw an angel who told him that one day people would come from another land. They would look strange but they would be good people, and they would bring good teaching; the people should listen and follow it. "That's why we were all waiting for you!" said Pedro.

Barbara and Russell were excited. Could it be

that God had been preparing these people to hear the gospel? They were full of anticipation as they set off to the village where Tiban lived. He was not there, but several other Tawbuid tribesmen arrived. They smiled and were friendly to the missionaries, but they found great difficulty in understanding them. Clearly, the dialects of the east were different from those in the west. They managed to talk a little, but there was no real contact.

The Reeds were disheartened as they returned home once more. Back in Ligaya, they met with more sadness: the cruel customs of animist religion had claimed another life. A young couple were expecting their first baby when the father met with an accident and died. As a result, the Tawbuid killed the baby at birth: they believed that a child born soon after the death of a family member would inherit a part of his soul. The village was, anyway, close to starvation – they had abandoned the fields of the men who had died of pneumonia because they must be unlucky. Then they had sold their entire rice harvest to buy ten pigs; all of these were sacrificed in a ceremony at the full moon, in an attempt to placate the spirits of the dead. Throughout the hours of darkness they took it in turns to rattle bamboo sticks together to scare away the spirits, yet the sound kept the whole village half-awake and uneasy: it was a constant reminder of what they feared. The missionaries felt depressed at their lack of success. They were surrounded by people living in misery, who listened to them with polite interest but whose hearts were unmoved by their words. They prayed urgently for release for their friends, for these kind, gentle, friendly people who could see no way out of the traps of oppression and fear which surrounded them.

## In God's time

A few months later, Jim Broomhall again encouraged them to make a trip across to the east. Obediently, Barbara and Russell packed up once again and trekked across the island. This time Caroline led them to a different village, where they were met by a group of smiling Mangyan people standing in front of a new house. Caroline explained that half of the palm-thatched house had been built by the Tadyawan, and half by the Tawbuid – an unheard of co-operation from a tribe who mixed very little with others. The group of Tawbuid was led by Tiban. He led the Reeds into the house and over to a six-foot wide platform about eighteen inches high, with a split bamboo floor – the place usually reserved for tribal leaders. Clearly, they were already held in high esteem.

Barbara and Russell had prepared carefully for their first meetings with the Tawbuid, but it was evident that they were to meet with a very different reception from usual. The people waited patiently while they unpacked their few belongings and supplies, and continued to sit expectantly at their feet: they were hoping that the missionaries would begin teaching them immediately. Russell took out his Bible, sat down on the platform, and began to talk. The Tawbuid listened eagerly and asked questions. Was this story really for them as well as for the white man? They told Russell that they already had a word in their language for a good spirit who created the world: *funbalugu*. Did this mean that the Good Spirit was more powerful than the spirits who ruled their lives?

Tiban told them more about his father's dream: "He told me that a new teaching would come into our tribal places in the jungle. When it came, I must listen and obey it. But only two weeks afterwards, he died. It is our custom to take this last order from my father as law, so when I heard about the women teachers, I came to find them. Tadyawan who spoke our language translated for me. Then I knew that we had to hear this teaching for ourselves."

Russell turned in his Bible to Acts 2:17, and read to him: "Your sons and daughters will prophesy, your young men will see visions, your old men will dream dreams." Surely that was what had happened among the Tawbuid!

It had not been easy for Tiban to come to the meeting place. The chief of his tribe had forbidden anyone to listen to the strangers, but Tiban was anxious to follow his father's instructions. In the end, he had killed three chickens for guidance: if they fell towards the interior, the people should stay in the jungle; if they fell towards the lowlands, they should go down to the river to listen to the teachers. One chicken fell towards the mountains, but two had fallen towards the lowlands, and so the Tawbuid had come.

The more the Reeds listened to the people, the more they understood how thoroughly their lives were ruled by the fear of the spirits. They saw that although they were intrigued by the idea of a God who loved them, much more fascinating to them was the fact of his power. A spirit who was more powerful than the demons could keep them safe! They began to teach them the stories of God's power and might, and gave them Bible verses to repeat when they were afraid, like Psalm 56:4: "In God I trust; I will not be afraid", or 2 Thessalonians 3:3: "The Lord is faithful, and he will strengthen and protect you from the evil one."

At last they felt that they had planted the seed in good ground, where it could take root and flourish. Family after family came to listen to them, to hear about the God who made the rocks and the rivers, the jungle and the mountain, the men and the women of all the tribes. They could see that a powerful Creator like that would have power even over the spirits – and they loved to hear that the Creator Spirit loved them and cared for them, and would never trick them or scare them. When they learned that they no longer needed to make sacrifices, they were happy, and when they learned how Jesus had been willing to sacrifice his life for them, they were amazed. What a wonderful God! They were ready to praise and thank him, and they were eager to learn the songs and stories that told how he loved them. Barbara and Russell were full of joy: after all their faithful waiting, a church was being born before their eyes.

## Changing ways

The Reeds settled in Safa, a village in eastern Mindoro. The church continued to grow, and some of the men had even walked across the mountain to help other tribal believers to build houses for the Bible school at Ayan Bekeg. For most of them, it was the first time they had met people from other tribes, and at first they were hesitant. Soon, however, they realised that they were all part of one family of believers, and they grew in confidence, praying and singing together. It was a major step forward in their understanding of their own society.

However, the old customs were hard to shake off, even among the Christians. One day, Barbara went to see her friend Linday, who had given birth to a baby girl the night before. Linday sat by the fire, leaning on a wooden back rest. The light was dim inside the smoky house, but Barbara could see that she was not holding her baby. After a moment, she caught sight of the child, lying naked and still on a rattan mat in a corner of the room. The placenta lay beside her, still attached to the baby by the uncut cord.

Barbara knew that the baby was almost two months premature, and guessed she was stillborn, but when she touched the child she found she was warm and breathing.

"What's wrong, Linday?" she asked. "Why aren't you holding her? And what's this yellow stuff on her head?"

"It's sweet potato," replied the mother. "It is our custom. It won't live; it came too early. It is better this way. When it is dead, I will sew up the mat and we will bury it in the jungle."

Barbara was horrified. Both parents were Christians, who worshipped in the little church in the village. They had longed for this baby and looked forward to her coming. But traditional wisdom said that a baby who was born early was unlikely to live (and no wonder, she thought angrily, if they are left exposed like this!). Rather than see the infant as a real person, whose spirit could come back to haunt them, it was better to treat it as a non-person, just part of the afterbirth expelled from the body and thrown away. Without thinking, they had gone along with the custom, even though they were both deeply sad.

Barbara drew a deep breath. "God made you and loves you," she said, "and he gave you this little one to love and cherish. He wants you to care for her."

Linday's husband got up from the corner where he had been sitting, sunk in gloom. "Do you mean that God wants us to love this thing?" he said. "Should we hold it? Might it live?"

"I think she will live," said Barbara. "I'll help

you to look after her." She went home and collected a cardboard box to protect the baby from draughts, some soft cloths, and a bottle filled with hot water and wrapped in a towel to keep her warm. It wasn't exactly an incubator, but it was the best they could manage. When she got back, the parents had cut the cord and were carefully cleaning the sweet potato from the baby's head. They tucked the baby into her new bed with the warm bottle, and then prayed together. Barbara asked for God's blessing on this little family, who were finding the courage to leave behind the old customs based on fear, and go forward in faith and trust.

## Opposition

Barbara and Russell carried on working among the new churches; their major task was to translate the New Testament into Tawbuid. They were a hidden and secretive people, who had almost no contact with outsiders. Few of them spoke any Tagalog, the Filipino language which enabled them to trade with the lowlanders, and few of them spoke any other tribal languages.

There were even some difficulties with the differences between the dialects of the eastern and the western Tawbuid.

However, the eastern Tawbuid were concerned for their brothers in the west, who had been so unresponsive to the missionaries for so long. They began to make trips of their own across the island, to tell the tribespeople how God had changed their lives. As a result, small churches were springing up there, too. They were not unopposed: the shamans – the "witch doctors" or "doctor priests" who worked by magic and sorcery – knew that their power was being eroded. In some places, they used poison on groups of believers, to reinforce the power of the spirits.

Land grabbing was also a problem. Lowlanders looked down on the illiterate Mangyan, with their simple way of life. They would take over areas the Tawbuid had cleared from the jungle to grow their own crops, and annexe them to their own farms, driving off the tribesmen with threats and beatings. The lumber men were also ruthless in pursuit of their trade, bulldozing the jungle and driving wide roads into the interior: logging was gradually deforesting whole mountainsides, as the slow-growing forests of ebony and mahogany were cut and sold overseas.

One day, a group of lumber men seized the Safa church as their headquarters, lighting camp fires, smoking cigarettes, shouting and laughing at the Tawbuid. Some of them grabbed at the young girls and tried to kiss them. The Tawbuid were a gentle people, unaccustomed to standing up for their rights, so they decided to pray together and ask God for help. Shortly afterwards, five days of torrential rain washed away the newly built roads, and brought the entire operation to a standstill. The lumber men left the church and never returned.

## Prophecy fulfilled

One of the faithful members of the Safa church was Suklinyan. He had taken his family and moved to a village in a remote mountain area, where the people were especially fearful of the spirits, hoping to tell them about the powerful Creator God. When he told Barbara that he, too, was experiencing opposition from the village leaders, she asked him what he intended to do. "I'll just keep living there and witnessing," he replied. "In God's time, the people will be ready to hear about him." Barbara thanked God for the steadfast courage and faith of people like Suklinyan, who cared so much for his brothers.

"Has anyone told you about the prophecy among our people that you would come with teaching for us?" he went on.

"Oh, yes, Tiban told us about his father's dream," Russell answered.

"Oh, it came many generations before Tiban's father. It was handed down from father to son for many years. Our fathers said that white teachers would come and we were to listen and obey their teaching. We would know who they were because the true teachers would be able to speak our language."

Russell and Barbara were shaken. As far as they knew, they were the only outsiders who had ever visited and learned Tawbuid. So that was the reason for all those years in the wilderness when they had felt like failures, when only their faith in

God's calling encouraged them to persevere: they had to learn the language so that they could speak to the Tawbuid in their own tongue, and fulfil the prophecy.

Like most people with an unwritten language, the Tawbuid relied on an oral tradition in which stories were passed from parents to children for generations, kept alive by constant repetition. They could also recite the names of their ancestors far back into the past. Suklinyan helped Barbara and Russell trace the prophecy back through sixteen generations – more than three hundred years.

"God must have had us on his mind a long, long time ago," said Suklinyan.

## Into the future

Barbara and Russell left Mindoro in 1994, still working on their Tawbuid New Testament. They left an island very different from the one they first knew. The Mangyan tribespeople have a new sense of dignity and worth, born of the knowledge that they are precious to God the Creator. No longer worried about pleasing unpredictable and malicious spirits, they have confidence in the power and love of God through Jesus Christ. Bringing the tribes together at believers' conferences and Bible schools has broken down ancient barriers of ignorance and mistrust between the tribes, enabling them to work together. This in turn has strengthened their position with the Philippine government, gaining them access to agricultural, medical and legal help. They have begun to get their land registered so that it can no longer be stolen from them, and the organisation of Mangyan churches has developed programmes to educate young people through secondary school and even college, but without destroying their traditional way of life.

In 1996 the Reeds completed their translation of the New Testament into Eastern Tawbuid, and Bibles were published by OMF and delivered to Mindoro by the Philippine Bible Society. In January 2000, a dedication ceremony was held for the Western Tawbuid New Testament, compiled by Derek and Liz Daniel, OMF missionaries from the UK. They were helped by three Tawbuid Christians: Sulian, one of the first believers and one of their main co-translators; Loreto, son of a powerful shaman, who helped with the editing and led the dedication ceremony; and Daniel, a young man from a Christian family who represented the younger generation who have no experience of the old animist religion.

The dedication included the performance of a play. Wearing only their loincloths and smeared with ash and clay, the Tawbuid re-enacted the arrival of the first missionaries forty years ago. There was laughter from the crowd of 500 people as they recalled how much they had feared the first Western visitors, and the spirits who had ruled their lives. Also in the audience was a group of non-believers, including a shaman. They were a visible reminder that the work of God goes on, taking the message of love and life to all his people – a people whose hearts were prepared long ago by visions and dreams of a new message and a new life.

# ENGLISH-SPEAKING OMF CENTRES

**AUSTRALIA:** P.O. Box 849, Epping, NSW 2121
Freecall 1 800 227 154
email: omf-australia@omf.net  *www.au.omf.org*

**CANADA:** 5759 Coopers Avenue, Mississauga ON,
L4Z 1R9
Toll free 1-888-657-8010
email: omfcanada@omf.ca  *www.ca.omf.org*

**HONG KONG:** P.O. Box 70505, Kowloon
Central Post Office, Hong Kong
email: hk@omf.net  *www.omf.org.hk*

**MALAYSIA:** 3A Jalan Nipah, off Jalan Ampang,
55000, Kuala Lumpur
email: my@omf.net  *www.omf.org*

**NEW ZEALAND:** P.O. Box 10-159, Auckland
Tel 09-630 5778   email: omfnz@compuserve.com
*www.nz.omf.org*

**PHILIPPINES:** 900 Commonwealth Avenue,
Diliman, 1101 Quezon City
email: ph-hc@omf.net   *www.omf.org*

**SINGAPORE:** 2 Cluny Road, Singapore 259570
email: sno@omf.net   *www.omf.org*

**SOUTHERN AFRICA:** P.O. Box 3080,
Pinegowrie, 2123
email: za@omf.net   *www.za.omf.org*

**UK:** Station Approach, Borough Green, Sevenoaks,
Kent, TN15 8BG
Tel: 01732 887299   email: omf@omf.org.uk
*www.omf.org.uk*

**USA:** 10 West Dry Creek Circle, Littleton, CO
80120-4413
Toll Free 1-800-422-5330   email: omf@omf.org
*www.us.omf.org*

*OMF International Headquarters:*
*2 Cluny Road, Singapore 259570*